Let's meet Mrs. Good and the Cedar Valley Kids™!

Mrs. Good™

"Hello, my name is Mrs. Good. Welcome to school. Our class is for children of all ages and stages of learning development. We all learn at our own pace. This information will take time to understand. Keep reading it over and over again. Let's be positive, listen, ask questions and make this adventure fun!

Are you ready to meet the Cedar Valley Kids™?"

Amy™

Ricardo™

Tatiana™

Peek-a-Blue™

Omar™

Bo™

Rafferty™

Visit us at
www.cedarvalleypublishing.com
and discover more about
Mrs. Good and

Let's say the alphabet!

Point to A and begin. Let's go slow.

UPPERCASE LETTERS

A B C D E F G H I J K L M
N O P Q R S T U V W X Y Z

lowercase letters

a b c d e f g h i j k l m
n o p q r s t u v w x y z

"Many children think L-M-N-O-P is one letter. Watch out!"

Let's mix up the alphabet!

Find the letters in your name. What other letters can you find?

UPPERCASE LETTERS

B D X K J I T H O Q P Z A
E N W M C G F R V U L Y S

lowercase letters

n q p t x o b d z s y m w c a
k h r g j i e v u f l

"It's easy to mix up
b with d, m with w,
i with j, p with q
and u with v.
Do your best!"

Let's say each word!

What is the first letter sound you hear? Big A, little a, **a-a** ant.

Aa ant

Bb bat

Cc cat

Dd dog

Ee egg

Ff fox

Gg goat

Hh hat

Ii igloo

Jj jam

Kk kite

"Can you say another word that starts with each letter?
Big A, little a, **a-a** apple."

Ll lion

Mm moon

Nn nut

Oo octopus

Pp pig

Qq queen

Rr rat

Ss sun

Tt turtle

Uu umbrella

Vv van

Ww watch

Xx x-ray

Yy yo-yo

Zz zebra

"Now, let's find the vowels a, e, i, o and u highlighted in green.
S-s super!"

Let's name colors!

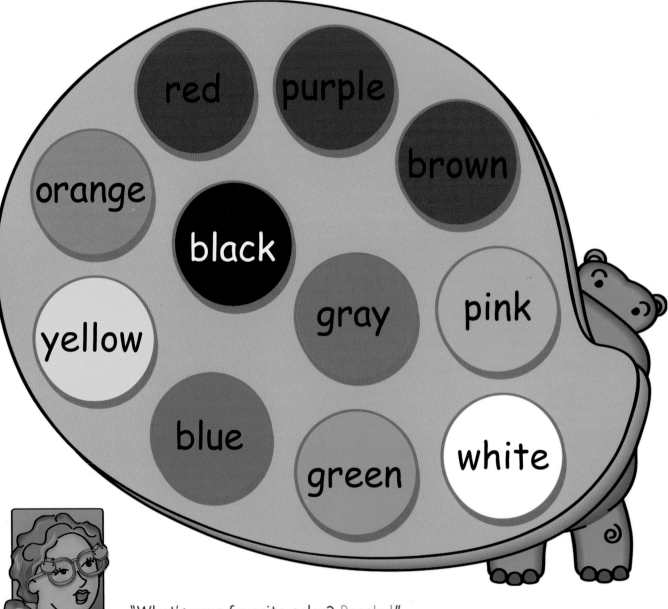

red

purple

brown

orange

black

yellow

gray

pink

blue

green

white

"What's your favorite color? Peachy!"

Let's name shapes!

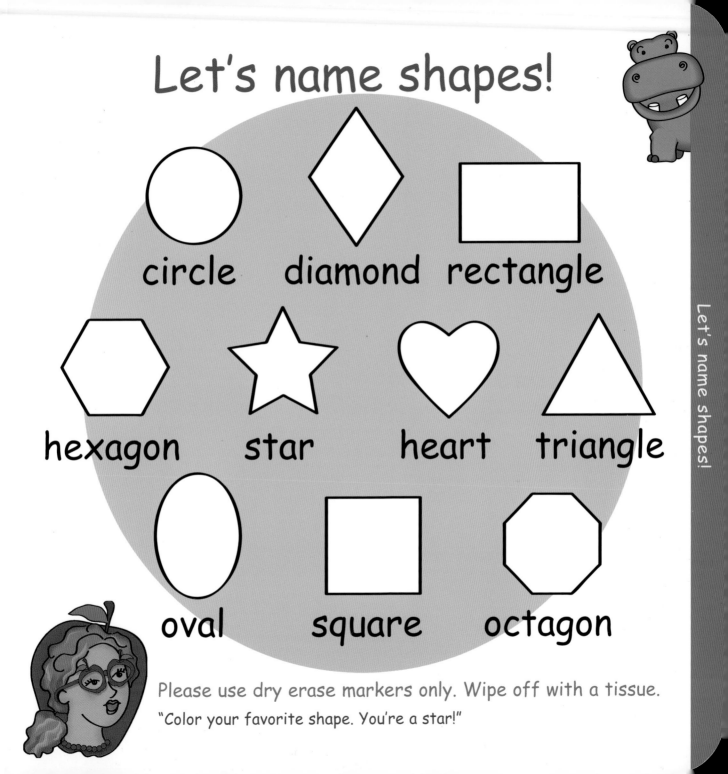

circle

diamond

rectangle

hexagon

star

heart

triangle

oval

square

octagon

Please use dry erase markers only. Wipe off with a tissue.

"Color your favorite shape. You're a star!"

Let's find your left hand!

middle   pointer or index

ring

pinky

thumb

"Your left hand makes an 'L'. Stupendous!"

Let's find your right hand!

pointer or index   middle

ring

thumb

pinky

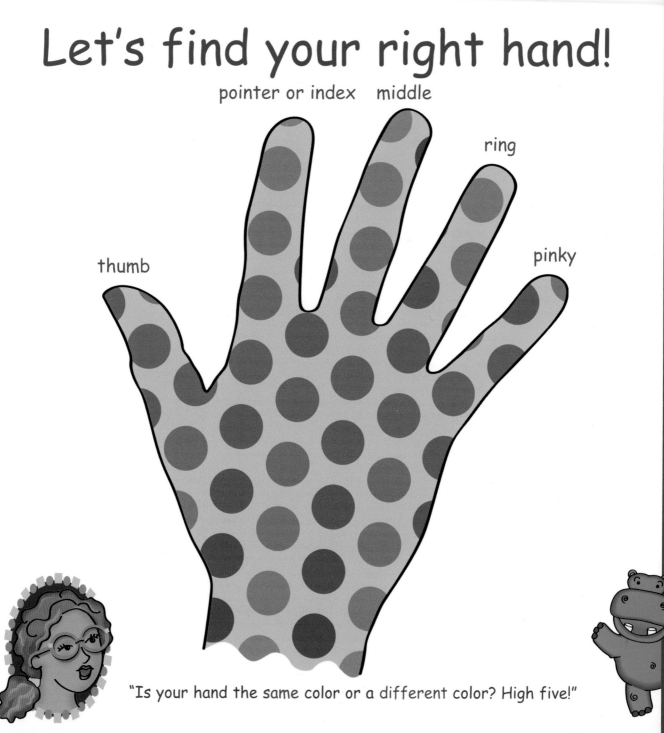

"Is your hand the same color or a different color? High five!"

Let's say some numbers!

Let's count!

0 1 2 3 4 5 6 7 8 9
10 11 12 13 14 15 16 17 18 19
20 21 22 23 24 25 26 27 28 29
30

"Can you find
15, 7, 18, 13, 9 and 17?
They're easy to miss
when learning to
count. Well done!"

Let's mix up some numbers!

How old are you? Can you find that number?
What other numbers can you find?

7 2 4 9 5 3 0 1 6 8

15 19 10 17 12 18 11 14 16 13

30 21 27 29 23 26 22 25 28 20

24

"Way to go!"

Let's count!

Did you know that numbers can be words?
Let's point and say each number and word.

0 zero

1 one

2 two

3 three

4 four

"Magnificent!"

5 five

6 six

7 seven

8 eight

9 nine

10 ten

Let's count to 100!

0	1	2	3	4	5	6	7	8	9
10	11	12	13	14	15	16	17	18	19
20	21	22	23	24	25	26	27	28	29
30	31	32	33	34	35	36	37	38	39
40	41	42	43	44	45	46	47	48	49
50	51	52	53	54	55	56	57	58	59
60	61	62	63	64	65	66	67	68	69
70	71	72	73	74	75	76	77	78	79
80	81	82	83	84	85	86	87	88	89
90	91	92	93	94	95	96	97	98	99
100									

"Can you count by 10s starting with zero?"

Let's skip count!

By 10s:

10 20 30 40 50 60 70 80 90 100

By 5s:

5 10 15 20 25 30 35 40 45 50

By 2s:

2 4 6 8 10 12 14 16 18 20

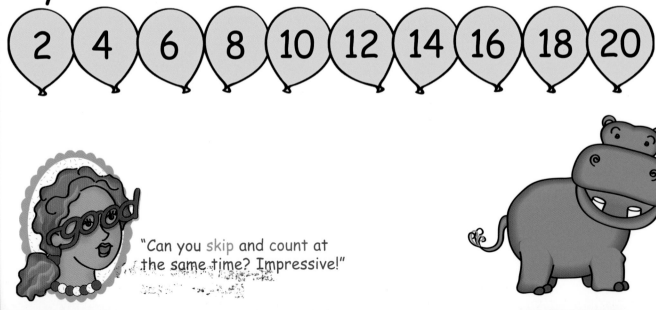

"Can you skip and count at the same time? Impressive!"

Let's look at money!

1¢   penny

5¢   nickel

10¢   dime

25¢   quarter

$1.00   dollar

"That makes a lot of cents!"

Let's say opposites!

big

little

fast

slow

hot

cold

happy

sad

"Can you name another pair of opposites? Terrific!"

Let's rhyme!

cat   hat

pig   wig

dog   log

jam   ham

"Open your ears so you can hear. The middle and ending sound make a rhyme. That's fine!"

Let's say positional words!

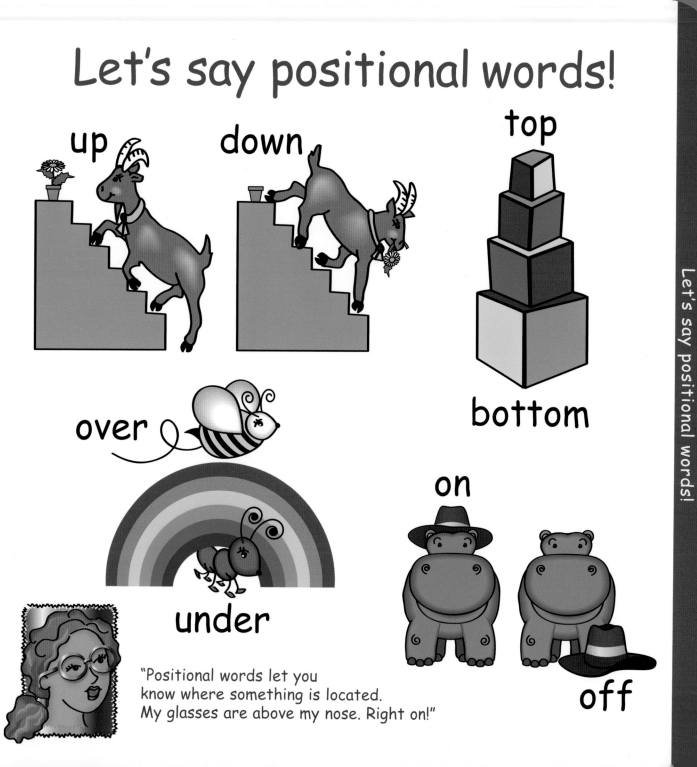

up

down

top

bottom

over

under

on

"Positional words let you know where something is located. My glasses are above my nose. Right on!"

Let's find your body parts!

head
eye
ear
nose
mouth
neck
chest
stomach
hip
heel
toe

finger
thumb
hand
arm
elbow
shoulder
back
knee
leg
ankle
foot

"You're head and shoulders above the rest!"

Let's name your five senses!

sight

sound

taste

smell

touch

"Hippo-licious!"

Let's learn more words!

the   a   **and**   I

is   **at**   in   not   on

that   he   like   me

to   **said**   are

have   **was**   you

we   it   can   go

be   did   for   want

make   look   **see**

"These are frequently used words.
Can you find some of these words on the next page?"

Let's read a story!
Hippo Plants a Seed
Author: I. M. Hippo

Hippo planted a seed. He watered the seed.
The seed grew into a beautiful flower.

Beginning	Middle	End
Hippo planted a seed.	He watered the seed.	The seed grew into a beautiful flower.

"Can you tell what happened in the beginning, middle and end?"

Let's tell time!

The short hand tells the hour. The long hand tells the minute. Let's point to the clocks and tell the time.

| 8 o'clock | 12 o'clock (noon) | 3 o'clock | 8 o'clock |

8:00 AM **12:00 PM** **3:00 PM** **8:00 PM**

| 8 o'clock | 12 o'clock (noon) | 3 o'clock | 8 o'clock |

"What do you do at 8:00 am, 12:00 pm (noon), 3:00 pm and 8:00 pm? Tick-tock, you rock!"

Let's make a calendar!

Let's say the months of the year. Let's say the days of the week.

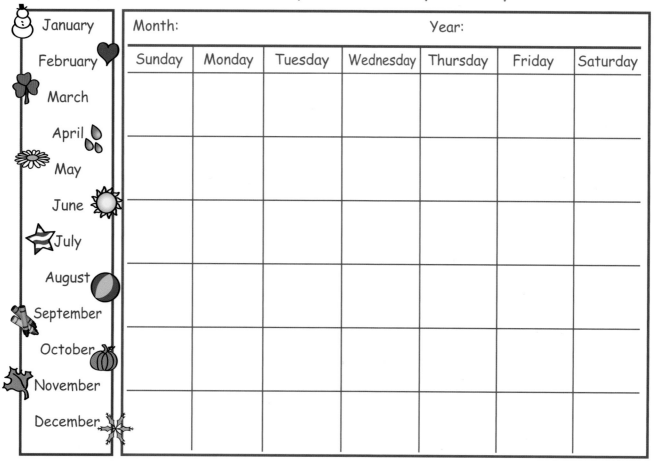

January	Month:					Year:	
February	Sunday	Monday	Tuesday	Wednesday	Thursday	Friday	Saturday
March							
April							
May							
June							
July							
August							
September							
October							
November							
December							

Please use dry erase markers only.
Wipe off with a tissue.

"Write in the month of your birthday. Now fill in the year and numbers to complete the calendar. Happy Birthday!"

Let's practice!

Do you know your full name? Let's say it.
Are you ready to write it?

Name

Do you know your address? Let's say it.
Are you ready to write it? Just ask if you need help.

Address

Do you know your telephone number?
Let's say it. Are you ready to write it?

Telephone Number

"Practicing with you is so much fun!"

Let's dial your telephone number!

Practice on our telephone page.

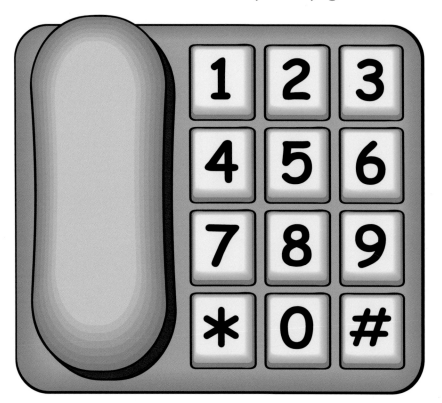

"Discuss how to use a real phone and what to do in an emergency. Thank you."

Let's doodle, silly noodle!

Let's look at the five stages of writing!

Drawing/Scribbling	• Drawing and scribbling with meaning
Random Letters	• Some scribbles that are beginning to look like letters
Copying Print	• Copying letters and words
Phonetic Spelling	• Printing the sounds heard and inventive spelling
Standard Spelling	• Moving from phonetic spelling to standard spelling

A p WLN

With ME muZEAM

Last night I went to Grandma and Grandpa's